JERMYN STREET THEATRE

Parents' Evening

by Bathsheba Doran

T0353529

European premiere at Jermyn Street Theatre
3 – 27 October 2018
Press performance Friday 5 October

PARENTS' EVENING

Premiered at the Jermyn Street Theatre, London on 3 October 2018 with the following cast:

CAST

Mother	Amy Marston
Father	Peter Hamilton Dyer

CREATIVE TEAM

Writer	Bathsheba Doran
Director	Stella Powell-Jones
Designer	Charlotte Espiner
Lighting Designer	William Reynolds
Sound Designer	Yvonne Gilbert
Stage Manager	Olivia Roberts
Production Manager	Will Herman
Production Photographer	Harry Livingstone

Produced and general managed by Jermyn Street Theatre.

With thanks to Nicole Buncher.

CAST

AMY MARSTON
Mother

Training: Bristol Old Vic.

Theatre includes: *Broken Glass* (Watford Palace Theatre); *Feed the Beast* (Birmingham Rep Theatre); *A Small Family Business*, *The Children's Hour* (National Theatre); *Stepping Out* (Salisbury Playhouse); *Man in the Middle* (Theatre 503); *Don John* (BAC/ Tour); *Humble Boy* (Northampton Theatre Royal); *Enlightenment* (Abbey Theatre Dublin); *After Mrs Rochester* (Shared Experience, West End); *Henna Night*, *Sitting Pretty* (Chelsea Theatre); *Ghost Train Tattoo*, *Snake in a Fridge*, *Snapshots*, *Unidentified Human Remains* (Royal Exchange Theatre, Manchester) and *Eurydice* (Whitehall Theatre).

Film includes: *Six From Eight*, *The Little Stranger*, *A Christmas Prince*, *The Current War*, *A Crown for Christmas*, *Toast*, *Personal Jesus*, *Bel Ami*, *The Imaginarium of Doctor Parnassus*, *The Mascot* and *Charlotte Gray*.

Television includes: *Summer of Rockets*, *Vera*, *Endeavour*, *EastEnders*, *Quacks*, *The Coroner*, *DCI Banks*, *New Worlds*, *Chickens*, *Frozen Addicts*, *Unforgettable Amnesiac*, *Consuming Passions*, *Kingdom*, *Doc Martin*, *Doctors*, *Heartbeat*, *Rome*, *The Last Detective*, *Jericho*, *Man/Woman*, *The Quest 3*, *He Knew He Was Right*, *Judge John Deed*, *Plain Jane*, *Mrs Bradley Mysteries*, *Where the Heart Is*, *Hello Girls*, *The Adventures of Tom Jones*, *The Black Velvet*, *Band*, *Neverwhere*, *Over Here*, *Casualty* and *Holby City*.

Radio includes: *Mr Spectator*, *The Number of the Dead*, *The Problem with Caves*, *The Running lady*, *Couples*, *David Copperfield*, *Mr Fieldings Scandal Shop* and *The Glass Wright*.

PETER HAMILTON DYER
Father

Theatre includes : *#WeAreArrested*, *Midsummer Night's Dream*, *Epicoene* (RSC); *Twelfth Night*, *King Lear*, *The Tempest*, *Antony and Cleopatra*, *Richard III*, *Henry VIII*, *Comedy of Errors*, *All's Well That Ends Well*, *The Changeling*, *The Broken Heart*, *Anne Boleyn*, *Holding Fire!*, *The Frontline*, *The Golden Ass* (Shakespeare's Globe); *Mrs Orwell* (Southwark Playhouse/ Old Red Lion); *Richard II* (Royal Exchange); *The Caretaker* (Dundee); *Miss Julie* (Southampton); *The Bacchae* (Shared Experience); *Mansfield Park* (Sheffield/Chichester); *Comfort Me With Apples* (Hampstead) and *One Flew Over The Cuckoo's Nest* (UK Tour).

Television includes: *Upstart Crow*, *EastEnders*, *Babs*, *Wolf Hall*, *Genius*, *Downton Abbey*, *Doctors*, *Silk*, *Silent Witness*, *Holby City* and *The Bill*.

Radio includes: *BBC Radio Rep*, *Book of the Week*, *Bournewood*, *Scribblers*, *The Colour of Milk*, *Pilgrim*, *Ulysses*, *Titanic*, *Mrs Dalloway*, *Black Dirt*, *Songs and Lamentations*, *The Lifeblood*, *The Tempest* and *Twelfth Night*.

CREATIVE TEAM

BATHSHEBA DORAN
Writer

Theatre includes: *The Mystery of Love and Sex* (Lincoln Center/ Signature Theatre); *Kin* (Playwrights Horizons); Parents' Evening (Flea Theater); *Ben and the Magic Paintbrush* (South Coast Repertory Theater) and *Feminine Wash* (Edinburgh Fringe Festival).

Television includes: *Jerusalem, The Looming Tower, Smash, Codes of Conduct, Masters of Sex, Boardwalk Empire*. She is currently show running JJ Abrams new show for HBO. Her own show, *Traitors*, will premiere on Channel 4 this January.

She is a 2009 recipient of the Helen Merrill Playwriting Award, three Lecomte du Nouy Lincoln Centre playwriting awards and a Susan Smith Blackburn Award finalist. She moved to the United States from the UK on a Fulbright Scholarship in 2000, received her M.F.A from Columbia University, and went on to become a playwriting fellow of The Juilliard School. This is her European premiere.

STELLA POWELL-JONES
Director

For Jermyn Street Theatre: *Tomorrow At Noon, The Play About My Dad*.

Other theatre includes: *The Healing* (TBTB, New York); *The Mystery of Love and Sex* (Signature Theater, VA); the West Coast Premiere of Nick Jones' *Trevor* (Circle X, Los Angeles); Stephanie DiMaggio and Anton Dudley's *12 Orchard Point* (Theater Row); *Robin Hood* (Williamstown Theatre Festival); plays by Lauren Morelli, Brian Watkins & Marco Ramirez for Lesser America's *Just Right Just Now*.

Associate directing credits: *The Father* (West End/National Tour).

Stella Powell-Jones is Deputy Director of Jermyn Street Theatre, funded by the Carne Trust. She recently returned to London after establishing a successful career in New York, where she directed new work by writers including Bathsheba Doran, Samuel D.Hunter and Nick Jones.

CHARLOTTE ESPINER
Designer

For Jermyn Street Theatre: *The Play About My Dad*.

Charlotte studied Classics at King's College, Cambridge before training in Set and Costume Design at the Motley Theatre Design School in 2011.

Other theatre includes: *Acis and Galatea* (St John Smith's Square); *Kingdom Come* (RSC); *Summerfolk* (Vanbrugh Theatre/RADA); *Home Chat* (Finborough Theatre); *Adler and Gibb* (Summerhall, Edinburgh/The Unicorn/The Lowry/Kirk Douglas Theatre, LA); *It is Easy to be Dead* – Olivier Award nomination (Finborough Theatre/Trafalgar Studios); *All or Nothing, The Musical* (West End/UK National Tour/Waterloo Vaults); *The Revenger's Tragedy* (Oval House Theatre); *Mouthful* (Trafalgar Studios); *The Devil to Pay on Brook Street* (Handel House Museum); *Pal Joey* (Karamel Club); *The Dispute* (Summerhall, Edinburgh/Odeon Cinemas); *The Winter's Tale* (Bernie Grant's Centre); *The Tempest* (Oval House Theatre);*This Child* (Bridewell Theatre); *Richard II* (St James' Church, Paddington); *Hamlet* (The Rose Theatre, Southwark); *The Provoked Wife* (Greenwich Playhouse); *Entries on Love* (RichMix) and *Abstract/Nouns* (Pleasance).

Film design credits include: *The Rain Collector* (Wigwam Films); *Lizard Girl* – BAFTA award winner (BBC); *Double Take* (BAFTA/Channel 4); *Paper Mountains* (Ruby Productions); *Copier* (Screen West Midlands Digishorts) and *Mirror* (Ruby Productions).

WILLIAM REYNOLDS
Lighting Designer

For Jermyn Street Theatre: *Stitchers*; *Blinding Light* (lighting); *Bloody Poetry* (set, video) and *Saturday Night* (set, lighting; also Theatre Royal Windsor & Arts Theatre).

Other theatre includes: *Trying It On* (lighting, video - RSC/ Royal Court/UK Tour); *Weimar Cabaret* (set, lighting - Barbican Theatre); *In the Willows* (set, lighting - Exeter Northcott/

UK Tour); *Sonnet Walks* (Globe Theatre); *Little Mermaid* (set, lighting - Theatre by the Lake/UK Tour); *Jungle Book* (set, lighting - London Wonderground/International Tour); *Blown Away* (set, lighting - Lyric Hammersmith/International Tour); *Radiant Vermin* (set, lighting - Soho Theatre/Brits Off Broadway); *Prima Donna* (video - Sadlers Wells) and *The Gambler* (video - Royal Opera House).

Upcoming designs include: *Smoke & Mirrors* (Aurora Orchestra). William is Artistic Director of Metta Theatre www.mettatheatre. co.uk and an Artist in Residence at the V&A Museum.

YVONNE GILBERT
Sound Designer

For Jermyn Street Theatre: *The Last Ones*, *Hymn to Love*.

Other theatre includes: *Giselle* (English National Ballet); *Shirley Manda* (Playground Theatre); *Moonfleet* (*Salisbury Playhouse*); *Rope* (Queens Theatre Hornchurch); *Oranges and Elephants* (Hoxton Hall); *I Loved Lucy* (The Arts Theatre); *Coming Clean* (Kings Head); *Urinetown* (The Pleasance); *Guess How Much I Love you* (Greenwich Theatre); *Murder Margret and Me* (York Theatre Royal); *Romeo and Juliet* (Rose Playhouse); *The Nativity* (St James Church); *Romeo and Juliet* (Theatre Clywd/New Theatre); *Much Ado about Nothing* (Rose Playhouse); *Brideshead Revisited* (York Theatre Royal); *Jacques Brel* (Mountview); *Ghost*, *On the Town*, *Addams Family Musical*, *Lift*, *Rent* (Ivy Arts Centre); *Man of La Mancha*, *Legally Blonde*, *American Idiot* (Bridewell Theatre); *Singer/Touched* (Bernie Grant Arts Centre); *Eighth Wonder of the World* (Brunel Museum); *Carousel* (Royal Academy of Music); *Twelfth Night* (Regents Park Open Air Theatre); *King James Bible*, *Statement of Regret* (National Theatre) and *Breed* (Theatre 503).

Associate credits include: *Macbeth* (Shakespeare's Globe); *Long Days Journey into Night* (Bristol Old Vic); *Peter and Alice*, *Privates on Parade* (Noel Coward Theatre); *A Chorus Line* (London Palladium); *Finding Neverland* (Leicester Curve); *Juno and the Paycock* (National Theatre).

JERMYN STREET THEATRE

During the 1930s, the basement of 16b Jermyn Street — close to Piccadilly in the heart of London's West End — was home to the glamorous Monseigneur Restaurant and Club. The space was converted into a theatre by Howard Jameson and Penny Horner in the early 1990s and Jermyn Street Theatre staged its first production in August 1994. The theatre director Neil Marcus became the first Artistic Director in 1995 and secured Lottery funding for the venue; the producer Chris Grady also made a major contribution to the theatre's development. In the late 1990s, the Artistic Director was David Babani, later the founder and Artistic Director of the Menier Chocolate Factory.

Over the last twenty years the theatre has established itself as one of London's leading Off-West End studio theatres, with hit productions including *Barefoot in the Park* with Alan Cox and Rachel Pickup, directed by Sally Hughes, and *Helping Harry* with Adrian Lukis and Simon Dutton, directed by Nickolas Grace.

Gene David Kirk, accompanied by Associate Director Anthony Biggs, became Artistic Director in the late 2000s and reshaped the theatre's creative output with revivals of rarely performed plays, including Charles Morgan's post-war classic *The River Line*, the UK premiere of Ibsen's first performed play *St John's Night*, and another Ibsen, *Little Eyolf* starring Imogen Stubbs and Doreen Mantle. Tom Littler staged two acclaimed Stephen Sondheim revivals: *Anyone Can Whistle*, starring Issy van Randwyck and Rosalie Craig, and *Saturday Night*, which transferred to the Arts Theatre.

In 2012 Trevor Nunn directed the world premiere of Samuel Beckett's radio play *All That Fall* starring Eileen Atkins and Michael Gambon. The production subsequently transferred to the Arts Theatre and then to New York's 59E59 Theatre. Jermyn Street Theatre was nominated for the Peter Brook Empty Space Award in 2011 and won The Stage 100 Best Fringe Theatre in 2012. Anthony Biggs became Artistic Director in 2013, combining his love of rediscoveries with a new focus on emerging artists and writers from outside the UK. Recent revivals include Eugene O'Neill's early American work *The First Man*, Terence Rattigan's first play *First Episode*, John Van Druten's First World War drama *Flowers of the Forest*, and a repertory season of South African drama. New works include US playwright Ruby Rae Spiegel's *Dry Land*, Jonathan Lewis's *A Level Playing Field*, and Sarah Daniels' *Soldiers' Wives* starring Cath Shipton.

Last summer, Anthony Biggs stepped down and Tom Littler took over as Artistic Director. Littler has previously been Associate Director of the new writing venue Theatre503 and Associate Director of the Peter Hall Company. He founded the theatre

company Primavera and ran it for over ten years, winning numerous awards. His opening production, the world premiere of Howard Brenton's *The Blinding Light*, was his sixth at Jermyn Street Theatre. Most recently Littler oversaw the most ambitious project in the theatre's history – the first complete London revival of Noel Coward's nine play cycle *Tonight at 8.30* since 1936. Jermyn Street Theatre's Deputy Director Stella Powell-Jones brought *Tomorrow at Noon* to the stage – three contemporary responses to Coward's work by female playwrights. The two productions ran side-by-side leading to 36 oneplays performed each week with tremendously popular trilogy days on Saturdays and Sundays. Throughout its history, the theatre's founders, Howard Jameson and Penny Horner, have continued to serve as Chair of the Board and Executive Director respectively, and the generous donors, front of house staff, and tireless volunteers all play their parts in the Jermyn Street Theatre story.

SUPPORT JERMYN STREET THEATRE

Everybody needs their best friends, and every theatre needs them too. At Jermyn Street Theatre we have recently started a Director's Circle. Limited to twenty- five individuals or couples, these are the people we rely on most. They sponsor productions, fund new initiatives, and support our staff. It is a pleasure to get to know them: we invite Director's Circle members to our exclusive press nights and parties, and we often have informal drinks or suppers in small groups. They are also an invaluable sounding board for me. Currently, members of the Director's Circle donate between £2,000 and £55,000 (with a threshold of £2,000 to join). They are our heroes and they make everything possible. We have space at the table for more, and I would love to hear from you.

Tom Littler
Artistic Director

THE DIRECTORS' CIRCLE

Anonymous
Michael and Gianni Buckley
Jocelyn Abbey and Tom Carney
Philip and Christine Carne
Colin Clark
Flora Fraser
Charles Glanville and James Hogan
Marjorie Simonds-Gooding
Peter Soros and Electra Toub
Martin Ward and Frances Card
Robert Westlake and Marit Mohn
Melanie Vere Nicoll

AT JERMYN STREET THEATRE

Find us at www.jermynstreettheatre.co.uk
@JSTheatre
Box Office: 020 7287 2875
16b Jermyn Street, London SW1Y 6ST

Jermyn Street Theatre is a charitable trust, Registered Charity No.1019755. It receives no regular statutory or Arts Council funding. Ticket sales account for around two-thirds of the costs of each production, with the remainder met through generous private donations, bequests, trusts and foundations, and corporate sponsorship. Subsidising our overheads and our productions requires around £300,000 each year.

PARENTS' EVENING

Bathsheba Doran

PARENTS' EVENING

OBERON BOOKS
LONDON

WWW.OBERONBOOKS.COM

First published in 2016 by Oberon Books Ltd

This single edition published in 2018 by Oberon Books Ltd
521 Caledonian Road, London N7 9RH
Tel: +44 (0) 20 7607 3637 / Fax: +44 (0) 20 7607 3629
e-mail: info@oberonbooks.com
www.oberonbooks.com

A catalogue record for this book is available from the British Library.

PB ISBN: 9781786826596
E ISBN: 9781786826602

Cover image: iStock

10 9 8 7 6 5 4 3 2 1

Parents' Evening was first produced by the Cherry Lane Theatre in New York as part of their Mentor Project on May 7, 2003. The performance was directed by Irina Brown, with costumes by Yvonne DeMoravia, lights by Brian Aldous, sound by Bart Fasbender, and props by Faye Armon. The Production Stage Manager was Kate Hefel. The cast was as follows:

MOTHER
Lisa Emery ....

FATHER
Ken Marks ....

Parents' Evening was later produced by the Flea Theater in New York on April 17, 2010. The performance was directed by Jim Simpson, with sets by Jerad Schomer, costumes by Claudia Brown, and lights by Brian Aldous. The Production Stage Manager was Carrie-Dell Furay. The cast was as follows:

MOTHER
Julianne Nicholson ....

FATHER
James Waterston ....

Characters

Mother (30s/40s)

Father (30s/40s)

Time and Place
Late 20th Century, a city.

Act One

The only thing that there needs to be on stage is a double bed. Anything else can be actual or suggested and should fade into the darkness of the rest of the stage, so that what we see is a small glimpse of a world floating in the island of the theatre.

The MOTHER has just come in the room. She is looking at some papers.

It is early evening.

FATHER: You were in with her for a long time.

MOTHER: She was upset.

FATHER: She was supposed to be upset. If she can't win gracefully then she shouldn't play.

MOTHER: She got excited.

FATHER: Oh so excited. Making up a little victory song. And then just singing it over and over again. 'I've won, you're dumb.' I mean that doesn't even rhyme.

MOTHER: It's a half rhyme.

FATHER: She took no pleasure in our company. Just wanted to roll over us like a fucking tank and win as quickly as possible.

MOTHER: The object of the game is to win, Michael.

FATHER: The object is to provide pleasant social interaction. That's what a game's for. That's why they were invented. They are meant to be a communal experience. Not an opportunity for our daughter to plot our destruction and then actually snort with glee once she's achieved it.

MOTHER: We ought to start her on Scrabble. It would be good for her vocabulary. And her spelling.

Beat.

FATHER: I'll tell you what I don't understand about Clue. Why would you kill someone with a candlestick, if there was a revolver available?

Beat.

I don't know. Gloating. It was disgusting. That is a bad habit.

MOTHER: I explained to her that it wasn't nice.

FATHER: For an hour?

MOTHER: No. And then we just talked.

FATHER: And what were you talking about?

MOTHER: She told me about her day.

FATHER: And how was her day?

MOTHER: She trespassed. On someone's property. During her lunch break.

FATHER: She what?

MOTHER: She went trespassing. I scolded her.

FATHER: Whose property?

MOTHER: I have no idea.

FATHER: She can't do that.

MOTHER: I know. That's what I told her.

FATHER: Jesus.

MOTHER: It's alright. She's consumed with guilt.

FATHER: That's all a big performance.

MOTHER: It wasn't a performance. By the time she told me she'd got herself so upset she could hardly breathe. But I calmed her down. We talked about it.

FATHER: I'm sure that's why she does these things. She does evil all day then pays penance in the evening and she knows perfectly well you'll absolve her. What did you do? Tell her to say a couple of Hail Mary's?

MOTHER: I told her not to do it again.

FATHER: That's it?

MOTHER: And I got her to talk about why she'd done it …

FATHER: And?

MOTHER: The other kids went.

FATHER: I don't like those kids she's hanging around with. That girl Victoria is a thug.

MOTHER: Her mother's a potter.

FATHER: Well her daughter's a criminal. Trespassing. Thank God they weren't caught. Were they?

MOTHER: Not as far as I know.

FATHER: I suppose the police would have contacted us by now.

MOTHER: I'll tell you who else wants to contact us.

FATHER: Who?

MOTHER: Sarah Barnes' mother.

FATHER: Oh God, what's Jessica done?

MOTHER: I don't know. Nothing. When Anne-Marie picked Jessica up from school today Mrs. Barnes told her to tell us that Jessica lent Sarah a book that apparently is inappropriate.

FATHER: Inappropriate how?

MOTHER: It was about sex.

FATHER: What does the woman want us to do? Censor Jessica's reading?

MOTHER: I know. I think it's fine, really. Jessica told me about it. It's teenage fiction. Young couple, they fall in love, they have sex.

FATHER: Well Jessica knows about sex.

MOTHER: And then they have oral sex.

Beat.

FATHER: Well she's read it now.

MOTHER: Yes, but it's one of a series.

FATHER: Oh.

MOTHER: She wants to read the rest of them.

FATHER: I see.

MOTHER: There are nine.

FATHER: Nine? What do they do by the end?

MOTHER: I have no idea.

FATHER: I wonder if we've done it …

MOTHER: The kids are hooked.

FATHER: I bet they are.

MOTHER: Mrs Barnes was upset. She wants to speak to us about it this evening.

FATHER: At least the kids are exchanging books. That's positive.

MOTHER: Not according to Mrs. Barnes. We'll have to spend the whole time avoiding her.

FATHER: I think we should tell her to fuck off. She can censor her own child's reading. I'm not censoring mine. And where does she get off communicating with us through the babysitter?

MOTHER: Do you really think we should let Jessica read them all?

FATHER: Yes. Who wrote them?

MOTHER: I don't know.

FATHER: They sound like crap.

MOTHER: They're not crap. They're educational. Now angel, I just have to finish this before we go.

The MOTHER goes back to her papers.

FATHER: Maybe I should see if Jessica wants to sign a peace treaty.

MOTHER: She's engrossed in book number three.

FATHER: Maybe we should buy her some D. H. Lawrence.

MOTHER: It's too hard.

FATHER: Look, I don't mind Jessica reading books with sexual content, but she should read good ones. Let's get her some D.H Lawrence.

MOTHER: It's too hard for her, Michael. She's ten!

FATHER: We could read it to her. Then if she has any questions …

MOTHER: I am not reading Jessica D. H. Lawrence.

FATHER: At least Lawrence is good.

MOTHER: He isn't very good, and he's extremely explicit.

The MOTHER goes back to her work.

FATHER: I think he's good. *(No response.)* Is there anything else I should know? So far we've covered her gloating, her increasing criminality and her filthy books.

The MOTHER looks up.

MOTHER: We talked about tonight.

FATHER: Is she nervous?

MOTHER: Slightly. She explained in great detail that Miss Broderick hates her, but it's not her fault.

FATHER: Which one's Miss Broderick?

MOTHER: The music teacher. Oh and Jessica gave me a form from her. She has to choose an instrument to play at school for next year.

FATHER: Really? That's nice. Is that something we're supposed to discuss with them this evening?

MOTHER: No. It's up to Jessica.

FATHER: What does she want to play?

MOTHER: Well she says trumpet.

FATHER: Oh fucking typical.

MOTHER: It's not terribly feminine. Not that it necessarily matters.

6

FATHER: Why can't she play the harp? Or what about the flute? Or the piano. What about the piano?

MOTHER: She wants to play the trumpet.

FATHER: It's all very well wanting to play the trumpet when you're ten. When you're thirty who cares? Unless you're actually a professional trumpeter.

MOTHER: It's what she wants.

FATHER: I think we should talk about this.

He waits until the MOTHER looks up from her papers.

It's a very important decision, Judy. What instrument she plays. I think she should play the piano or something.

MOTHER: Then talk to her about it.

FATHER: Do you think she should play the piano?

MOTHER: I don't really care, Michael. I think she should play whatever she wants.

FATHER: What about the violin?

MOTHER: No way. I refuse to listen to her scratching out tunes on a violin for the next five years. It would be unbearable. Not that the trumpet's going to be much better.

FATHER: When do we have to hand in the form?

Pause.

MOTHER: I don't know. Next week?

FATHER: I'll talk to her about the piano.

FATHER: I think she's quite musical.

MOTHER: As she demonstrated tonight with her little song.

FATHER: The song was unpleasant. But the impulse was creative. That's good. Maybe she'll become a great artist.

MOTHER: Well I tell you, she can't paint. A client came in the other day, noticed one of Jessica's pictures in my office, and assumed she was five. I didn't say anything.

FATHER: Five?

MOTHER: Five.

FATHER: Look, I know she can't paint. You're the one who's always telling her she can.

MOTHER: I'm being encouraging.

FATHER: It just makes her arrogant. She holds up a piece of paper she's been splashing paint on for two minutes, says 'it's good isn't it,' and you say 'yes.' I think we need to convey to her that a piece of art doesn't take two minutes.

MOTHER: It's alright, darling. You've made it very clear that it takes at least ten years.

FATHER: You know I do write all day. I don't just sit here and do nothing. And I don't bring it straight to you and say 'it's good, isn't it.' I mean, really …

MOTHER: What am I supposed to say to her? That it's bad?

FATHER: I did.

MOTHER: When?

FATHER: The other day. She said 'it's good isn't it,' I said 'no,' she said 'why,' I said 'because it's taken you two minutes.' She tried again. It was slightly better. I said so.

Beat.

MOTHER: Did you say it was "slightly better" or "better?"

FATHER: Better. I said it was better.

The MOTHER returns to her papers.

I told her I liked that poem though, didn't I? I thought that was wonderful. Really wonderful.

MOTHER: I know you did.

FATHER: Didn't you?

MOTHER: No, I thought it was awful.

FATHER: What?

MOTHER: What? It was.

FATHER: Judy, it was brilliant.

MOTHER: It didn't make sense.

FATHER: It did make sense. 'All's quiet, everyone's working. The only sound is of pencils writing.' There's real rhythm to that.

MOTHER: How can all be quiet if the only sound is of pencils writing?

FATHER: Because 'quiet' doesn't necessarily mean no sound. *(Whispering.)* This is quiet.

Beat.

I thought it was exceptional. I xeroxed it.

Beat.

Will you read it again?

MOTHER: Yes.

FATHER: But will you? I've stuck it to my filing cabinet.

MOTHER: Yes Michael. But right now I have to finish this.

The MOTHER works. The FATHER looks into his closet to select his clothes for the evening.

FATHER: Why you want me dressed up for this I have no idea. It just makes me more tense.

The FATHER stares into his closet.

What would you like me to wear?

MOTHER: A suit.

FATHER: Right. This is absolutely ridiculous.

MOTHER: I don't want to go either, Michael.

FATHER: I hate schools. They're such fascist institutions. They always make you feel like you're going to get into trouble.

MOTHER: Last year you did get into trouble. You made the history teacher cry.

FATHER: Because that wall display was bullshit!

MOTHER: It wasn't bullshit.

FATHER: Judy it was total bullshit. The "olden days." When were they? What time period exactly is the time period of horses and carriages and lots of vegetables in baskets?

MOTHER: Michael it was designed for people less than a decade old.

FATHER: No dates. Not a single date. It's a history display! We've got a ten year old in the house who thinks the past is just something that happened in black and white with wagons.

MOTHER: It's a gradual process. Next year they do the Civil War.

FATHER: And that will just be lots of pictures of soldiers and cannons and some poems by Whitman which no one will mention are homoerotic. Let's just see, let's just see, if she knows the dates of the war by the end of the year. I bet she doesn't. I bet the history teacher doesn't know them. I'm extremely tempted to quiz the stupid woman tonight. You remember when I asked her the date of the Boston Tea Party? No idea!

MOTHER: Michael, don't make a scene again.

FATHER: I wasn't going to make a scene. I was just suggesting a little quiz.

MOTHER: Well don't. Don't do anything.

FATHER: We are supposed to be discussing our daughter's education. That's why we're going.

MOTHER: I know but I don't want to be in there for a long time.

FATHER: Judy, this is important.

MOTHER: You know I find these evenings really nerve-wracking. It's bad enough waiting to see how many people are going to tell us that Jessica's a bad influence without worrying that you're going to attack the teachers. Alright?

FATHER: Come on. Everyone knows how bright Jessica is.

MOTHER: It's never about being bright. It's about behavior.

FATHER: Exactly. And that is what's wrong with the way they teach. If Jessica was actually busy learning things she's perfectly capable of, like dates, instead of doing quite so much coloring in, then there wouldn't be time for behavior. Of course she's disruptive. She's bored.

MOTHER: Well let's pray she's been less bored this year because I don't think I can bear another parade of teachers telling us that Jessica's not the only child in the class. God it was embarrassing.

FATHER: I thought they embarrassed themselves.

MOTHER: Perhaps I would have been less embarrassed if I hadn't been fairly sure that while you were making the history teacher cry, the entire room was watching, thinking 'no wonder Jessica's a bad influence, her parents are crazy.'

FATHER: You think they blame us?

MOTHER: Of course they blame us.

FATHER: *(A joke.)* Do they accept no responsibility for her delinquency? *(The MOTHER doesn't react.)* And we're not crazy.

MOTHER: It doesn't matter what we think, does it? It matters what they think.

FATHER: Come on … Don't get worked up. I think together we can handle a gaggle of grade school teachers. Especially all dressed up.

MOTHER: I'm not getting worked up, Michael. I want to finish this.

Beat.

It will take fifteen minutes. Then I'll get ready and we'll go. Alright? All I need now is my green file.

She starts looking through her papers. She looks up, body tensed.

I can't find it. Shit. It's green.

FATHER: Green file.

MOTHER: It's got everything in it.

FATHER: Have you left it downstairs?

MOTHER: It's not downstairs.

FATHER: Sorry.

MOTHER: Shit.

FATHER: It might be downstairs.

MOTHER: If I've lost it I'm in big trouble.

FATHER: You didn't lose it. You never have.

MOTHER: *(Searching.)* I wonder if I left it at work.

FATHER: Did you take it into the bathroom?

MOTHER: Why would I take it into the bathroom? Michael, you're in the way.

FATHER: Jessica's room? Well if you lost it there it's gone forever.

MOTHER: *(Searching.)* Not now, Michael.

FATHER: Fine. But I am going downstairs to enjoy a glass of wine before we leave and maybe, just maybe while I'm sipping it all my myself, I'll spy your green file, buried somewhere beneath the day's debris. *(No response.)* I think I saw a yellow file in the living room.

MOTHER: It's not a yellow file, Michael. It's green! It's my green file!

FATHER: What's the yellow one?

MOTHER: They're my files, Michael. Alright? Just let me think.

FATHER: Why do you scatter them all over the house? Between you and Jessica …

MOTHER: Yes, I know. We're a terrible disappointment to you.

FATHER: You're not a disappointment to me. I just feel like I'm drowning in everyone else's shit. I mean there are papers all over the house. No wonder you can't find anything.

MOTHER: You are not helping.

FATHER: Well let's clean up around here. I mean those photos of Spain have been piled on the mantelpiece for six months, Judy. You promised we were going to put them in an album. When are we going to do it?

MOTHER: I don't know.

FATHER: It just gets depressing. I feel like I spend the whole day wandering through our home sorting through papers I don't know what to do with because they're not mine, and switching off all the lights that Jessica has somehow managed to leave on in every single room in the one hour she has between getting up and going to school. I actually said to her this afternoon 'when you have your own house and you pay the electricity bill, then you can leave the lights on.'

The MOTHER stops her search.

MOTHER: You said that?

FATHER: It's a waste of money.

MOTHER: That is so stupid. That is such a cliché.

FATHER: And our electricity bill is ridiculous. What do you want me to do?

Pause. The MOTHER carries on searching.

FATHER: What if I showed Jessica the electricity bill? We could combine it with long division. How many times would her allowance go into the electricity bill?

MOTHER: Long division makes her cry.

FATHER: Yes, but she needs to learn how to do it and this could be a fun little exercise.

MOTHER: I can't find it. I'll have to finish this, go into work early, and hope to God I left it on my desk.

FATHER: Right. How early?

MOTHER: Early. And on debris, Michael.

FATHER: Debris. Tell me.

MOTHER: You have to flush condoms down the toilet.

FATHER: I can't. It gets clogged. Why?

MOTHER: Because Jessica saw one in our waste basket last week.

FATHER: She what!

MOTHER: She saw one in our waste basket and it upset her.

FATHER: Oh God.

MOTHER: So don't put them in there. Also, it's not nice.

FATHER: What did she say?

MOTHER: She said what's that?

FATHER: And what did you say?

MOTHER: I said that's Daddy's condom.

FATHER: You said it was mine?

MOTHER: It was yours. What did you want me to say?

FATHER: It was ours.

MOTHER: Fine. Next time.

FATHER: And I'm not going to feel fucking ashamed for making love to you! *(No response.)* And she shouldn't just walk in here without knocking.

MOTHER: She did knock. And I hate it.

FATHER: What?

MOTHER: The knocking. It's not natural.

FATHER: Politeness isn't natural. Neither is polished wood, or penicillin or pencil sharpeners but they all make the world a little more bearable.

MOTHER: Knocking on our door like a stranger.

FATHER: What if I'm getting changed?

MOTHER: Well she's already seen your condom.

FATHER: She's knocking on the door.

MOTHER: I told her that when I'm here she doesn't have to knock.

FATHER: Judy, that's not fair.

MOTHER: I don't think it's right that she knocks.

FATHER: What if we knock on her door too? Then it's a mutual respect situation. We respect her space. She respects ours.

MOTHER: I am not knocking on my child's door.

FATHER: I bet she'd like it. We'd be treating her like an adult.

MOTHER: She's not an adult.

FATHER: She is. She's a little adult.

MOTHER: Little adults are dwarves, Michael. She is a child.

Beat.

FATHER: Shall I bring you up a glass of wine?

*The MOTHER shakes her head. She's working. He looks at her.
A moment.*

I called the painters. They're coming on Monday.

MOTHER: Good.

FATHER: I didn't tell you, I spoke to my publishers. They're
extending my deadline.

Beat.

So I've got another six months.

MOTHER: Good.

FATHER: I can do it in six months. I just have to figure out
how to get Helena over to Portugal. I mean she's there.
I've got thirty pages of her in Portugal, having lunch, and
talking about Art as Philosophy. And it's very good, right?
We agreed I need to keep that section. She has to be there
for the lunch at the villa. But why would she suddenly up
and go to Portugal? *(Beat. He gasps.)* What if it's because
she knows David? *(Then, deflated.)* No, she can't know
David before the lunch. Otherwise I'd have to rewrite
that walk they have in the orange grove. Oh I don't know.
Maybe I should just cut the whole thing.

MOTHER: Michael, I have to do this! Now! We agreed if I came
home early you'd leave me time to do this. And since I got
home from work I've had to play a fucking board game,
calm you and Jessica down, listen to her catalogue of wrongs,
listen to your catalogue of complaints about your house, your
wife and your child, and now, twenty minutes before we
have to go out, you want me to talk about the fucking novel!
I've got to be in court tomorrow. I have to read this.

Beat.

17

FATHER: Maybe I'll drink some wine and listen to some jazz.

The phone rings. The MOTHER answers.

MOTHER: Hello? Oh, hi … Oh fantastic! That's fantastic.

FATHER: I thought you had to work.

The MOTHER ignores him.

MOTHER: Oh Ken, you're an angel!

He stands looking at her.

MOTHER: Oh thank God. Thank you. Thank you … No,
just bring it in tomorrow. It's fine, I'm going out tonight
anyway … yes, it's Parents Night at the school. I know,
I'm terrified. One of the mothers wants to kill us because
Jessica's been handing out dirty books …

She laughs at whatever he's saying on the other end.

They didn't … what did Lisa say? That's ridiculous … Oh
is she better?

The FATHER sighs heavily.

MOTHER: What did the doctor say?… Oh that's good …
We're fine …

The FATHER sighs again, looking at her.

I – no I … I'm sorry, Ken, I have to go. Yes. Yes. I will.
See you tomorrow … Thanks.

She hangs up. Beat.

FATHER: Wine and jazz. Off I go.

MOTHER: You have to let me talk on the phone, Michael.

FATHER: I do let you talk on the phone.

MOTHER: No you don't.

FATHER: Of course I do.

MOTHER: Then what was that?

FATHER: You said you were going to work.

MOTHER: Yes I know, but the phone rang.
And anyway that was work. Ken found my file.

FATHER: Great. Good for Ken.

MOTHER: Michael, I mean it. I really can't bear it when you do that.

FATHER: Do what?

MOTHER: When you look at me like that while I'm on the phone. I can't talk to anybody.

FATHER: Oh come on.

MOTHER: People comment on it. They're scared to call me here.

FATHER: What are you talking about? People call you all the time.

MOTHER: They don't, Michael.

FATHER: They –

MOTHER: I'm sorry, but they just don't!

FATHER: Judy …

MOTHER: They don't call me here! They don't!

FATHER: Someone just called!

MOTHER: Everyone at work is always taking about how scary it is calling me here. It's a joke. It's an office joke!

FATHER: Who makes jokes about it?

MOTHER: I'm not telling you who.

FATHER: Just tell me.

MOTHER: No.

FATHER: I don't believe it!

MOTHER: You don't hear yourself. You sound unbelievably irritated every time someone asks for me. You sigh at them!

FATHER: I am irritated. They're interrupting.

MOTHER: Interrupting what?

FATHER: We're talking, the phone rings, you start talking to someone else!

MOTHER: What am I supposed to do?

FATHER: Look, if you and I were in the middle of a conversation, and a passerby just walked up and joined in, that wouldn't be acceptable would it? That's what it's like. You should just say …

MOTHER: What? I can't talk now. My husband, who I talk to for at least ten hours a day, is finishing a point?

FATHER: Just tell them you're busy.

MOTHER: I'm not busy.

FATHER: Oh thank you very much.

MOTHER: Michael we live with each other. We can talk to each other all the time.

FATHER: No we can't, that's the whole point. We work all day, there's Jessica, there's everything else, then you've got work to do in the evening, sometimes I've got work to do in the evening. I mean we do not talk to each other for ten hours a day. Not even … not even … *(He does a mental calculation.)* Not even four, really.

MOTHER: I've never met a man who wants to talk so much. Talk talk talk talk talk, all the time.

FATHER: This is a marriage.

MOTHER: Yes, but you didn't contract a permanent companion.

FATHER: That is the definition of marriage.

MOTHER: I mean you even talk to me when I'm on the toilet.

FATHER: Oh I'm sorry. I thought that was a special intimacy that we shared.

MOTHER: Everyone does it! I've got Jessica telling me about her homework while I'm trying to poo, Michael.

FATHER: Jessica does it?

Beat.

MOTHER: Michael. I can't be your special friend all the time.

FATHER: Why not?

MOTHER: I do need some time to myself.

FATHER: You do have time to yourself.

MOTHER: When?

FATHER: On the way to work. At work. At lunch with all of your lawyer friends. Sitting all together in the sun eating ridiculously overpriced sandwiches and discussing who's in, who's out, and whatever else is new on the Rialto. Don't you? Every day.

MOTHER: Michael, I'm allowed other friends. You have friends.

FATHER: Not that are just mine.

MOTHER: You do, Michael.

FATHER: Very few.

MOTHER: What about Lewis?

FATHER: That's one.

MOTHER: And Eric.

FATHER: I never see him.

MOTHER: That's not my fault. He lives in Hawaii.

FATHER: Anyway, I think of them as our friends.

MOTHER: Well they're not. I have absolutely nothing in common with them.

FATHER: You get along very well with Lewis …

MOTHER: I think he drinks too much. But he's your friend. And I don't mind. Be friends with Lewis. Go away on special weekends to Jazz festivals in New Orleans with Lewis. Something I don't do with my friends. But please, just occasionally, would you let me speak to them on the telephone?

FATHER: I went away for one weekend.

MOTHER: The same weekend the dishwasher broke. It was a nightmare.

FATHER: Alright. I have Lewis. But you have lots of people.

MOTHER: I need lots of people, Michael. It's something I need. You don't like most people.

FATHER: I like you.

MOTHER: I know. And I like you.

Beat.

But now I have to work.

She picks up her papers. She starts reading them. Silence. The FATHER checks his watch. She notices. He shrugs helplessly.

FATHER: We don't want to be late …

She throws them down. She gets up and begins to get ready. Silence.

MOTHER: I hate these things. I really don't want to go.

FATHER: It will only take a couple of hours.

MOTHER: I'm working when we get back.

FATHER: Right.

MOTHER: And you're not to interrupt me.

FATHER: Judy, I go out of my way to accommodate you working. It's just that right before a Parent Teacher Conference isn't the best time, is it? You spent an hour with Jessica. And now we have to go.

MOTHER: I wouldn't have been with Jessica for an hour if you hadn't screamed at her.

FATHER: I wouldn't have screamed at her if she wasn't so incredibly badly behaved.

MOTHER: Screaming at her doesn't do anything.

FATHER: I'd have screamed some more if I'd known she spent the afternoon trespassing. Instead of telling her it was fine.

MOTHER: I didn't tell her it was fine.

FATHER: You shouldn't have gone in there at all. She was supposed to be in trouble. That child is getting completely out of control.

MOTHER: No she's not.

FATHER: Oh come on, Judy. Even the other parents want to talk to us about her.

MOTHER: One woman. One parent.

FATHER: Who next? One very angry homeowner who wants to know why she's crushed all of his fucking daffodils? And all you do is sit at the end of her bed swapping secrets for an hour.

MOTHER: I think it's better than losing my temper every five minutes.

FATHER: You shout at Jessica.

MOTHER: Not like you do. You hit her.

FATHER: I occasionally spank her and you do too.

MOTHER: Hardly ever.

FATHER: Because you don't have the energy. So I have to fucking deal with it. And then you throw it back in my face and act as though I were some terrible monster.

MOTHER: No I don't. But I have to put a considerable amount of energy into convincing Jessica that you aren't!

FATHER: That's very good of you. Much appreciated.

MOTHER: You scare her Michael.

FATHER: Well tough eggs! When a fucking tank rolls over me I'm not going to lie down!

MOTHER: I'll tell you what she does when you're shouting at her. She says to herself over and over again 'it doesn't matter.'

FATHER: What?

MOTHER: That's what she told me.

FATHER: No respect for me. It's amazing.

Beat.

Well that explains a lot.

MOTHER: It's a coping strategy.

FATHER: It explains why she just stood there staring at me with this big 'fuck you' look in her eyes.

MOTHER: That's exactly what I'd be thinking if someone called me a tank.

FATHER: You're not a tank. She is.

MOTHER: Which earrings?

FATHER: Those ones.

MOTHER: Michael, she does respect you.

FATHER: That song was pretty nasty, Judy.

MOTHER: We both agreed it wasn't any good at all.

FATHER: She thinks her father's stupid and a monster.

MOTHER: She doesn't, Michael. I explained to her that you're tense about the book.

FATHER: Oh right, I see, you think tonight was my fault.

MOTHER: I think you overreacted.

FATHER: Is that what the two of you were whispering about? My multiple failings? No wonder you took so long.

MOTHER: No, I just told her that the two of you had very different personalities.

FATHER: She's ten. Are you seriously telling me she's right?

MOTHER: You overreact, Michael. You sent her to her room for beating you at Clue!

FATHER: That is not why I sent her to her room and you know it!

MOTHER: You overreacted.

FATHER: Then why didn't you say anything?

MOTHER: Because you told me to keep out of it! I am not supposed to undermine you in front her!

FATHER: You do undermine me! You go straight in there and leave me sitting on the sofa like a fucking lemon.

MOTHER: She was upset!

FATHER: She knew she was way out of line. Until you told her it was all my fault.

MOTHER: I didn't!

FATHER: What about supporting me?

MOTHER: I'm not supporting anyone.

FATHER: I'm glad that's out in the open.

MOTHER: If I want to spend quality time with Jessica on the night of her Parent Teacher Conference then I will. What are you going to do about it?

FATHER: You know if you keep pretending that you and Jessica have a special relationship that doesn't include me, then you and Jessica will have a special relationship that doesn't include me.

MOTHER: It's impossible to talk to you when you're like this.

FATHER: You see? This is what you're like in conflict. You give up.

MOTHER: Michael. I'm a lawyer. My job is conflict.

FATHER: Yes, I know you're very good at your job dear but when it comes to –

MOTHER: Don't you dare!

FATHER: It doesn't help anything if you hide away with Jessica!

MOTHER: We weren't hiding. You could have come in.

FATHER: She didn't want me there!

MOTHER: What did you expect?

FATHER: I expected you to come back out! I had poured us both a glass of wine! You've got time for Ken, you've got time for Jessica, I'm just who you fit in between telephone calls!

MOTHER: That's not true.

FATHER: It is true! The priorities are work, Jessica, me.

MOTHER: Why do you have to put it in an order like that? That's not how it works.

FATHER: Because everything has an order. Everyone has priorities. And I am not yours. Do you ever wish you could spend more time with me?

MOTHER: Michael, we –

FATHER: I wish I could spend more time with you. Every day. And if I could, you wouldn't want it, would you?

MOTHER: I would if I didn't have anything else to do.

FATHER: Oh that's very comforting.

MOTHER: Oh Michael. Come on. I love you.

Pause.

Come on. I love you.

Beat.

I love you.

Beat.

Don't I?

Beat.

Yes I do. You're who I come home to.

FATHER: No, you come home to -

MOTHER: No. In here. You're who I come home to.

Beat.

FATHER: Yes?

MOTHER: Of course. But you have to know that. I can't perform it for you all the time.

FATHER: You're not going to leave me for Ken then?

MOTHER: Don't be absurd.

FATHER: Maybe I could marry Lisa. Who'd get Jessica?

MOTHER: Jessica loves you very much. You know that. Of course she's impossible. She's your daughter.

The FATHER smiles.

But sometimes she can be very sweet, can't she?

FATHER: Yes.

MOTHER: And she's very bright.

FATHER: And freakishly good at Clue.

MOTHER: She'll be alright.

She looks at herself in the mirror.

FATHER: You're beautiful.

MOTHER: Thank you.

FATHER: Are you ready?

MOTHER: I'm ready.

Beat.

Now, you realize we're going to have to think of something to say to Sarah Barnes's mother about the books.

FATHER: We'll think in the car.

MOTHER: Good.

FATHER: Now don't be nervous.

MOTHER: I'm not nervous. Be polite.

FATHER: Judy, would you please remember that it's not us they're assessing.

Beat.

MOTHER: Switch off the light.

They exit, turning out the light.

Act Two

A few hours later. Quiet in the bedroom for a moment. Then the parents return.

MOTHER: Would you just keep your voice down? Jessica's asleep.

FATHER: No I won't keep my fucking voice down. This is outrageous.

MOTHER: I know.

FATHER: I still cannot believe the way that teacher spoke to us. Have you ever heard anything like it?

MOTHER: No. No I haven't.

FATHER: She was so patronizing. 'If you'd just calm down for a moment ...' Calm down. Telling me to calm down. After insulting us.

MOTHER: Well insulting me, actually.

FATHER: Both of us. I think it's unbelievable. How old was she? Twenty-three? I will be writing a letter. Tomorrow. I think it's very interesting that they wouldn't let us see the principal tonight!

MOTHER: He wasn't there.

FATHER: Well he should have been there!

The FATHER looks at her.

Are you alright? What can I get you?

MOTHER: No I'm not alright.

FATHER: I'm going to kill Jessica.

MOTHER: Michael, that's not going to help.

FATHER: This is outrageous. Look at you.

MOTHER: Do I look white?

FATHER: You do.

MOTHER: I went white. When she said it I felt myself go completely white. Did you see?

FATHER: I thought you handled it so well.

MOTHER: Really?

FATHER: Yes. Phenomenally well.

MOTHER: I did stay very calm.

FATHER: You were amazingly calm. I thought I was going to kill her.

MOTHER: So did I.

FATHER: No, but you were amazing. Just got us out of there.

MOTHER: What are we going to do?

FATHER: We're going to talk to Jessica.

MOTHER: I want to talk to her by myself.

FATHER: Oh no. I want to talk to her.

MOTHER: Will you please let me handle this?

FATHER: No. I think we should handle this together.

MOTHER: No, you'll just shout at her.

FATHER: Damn right I'll shout at her. I won't have her talk that way about you.

MOTHER: I'm talking to her by myself.

FATHER: Absolutely not. Not this time.

MOTHER: I need to.

FATHER: No. You'll just let her walk all over you. I won't have it! She's in big trouble.

MOTHER: All she said was "I never see my mother."

FATHER: Yes and it's a fucking lie!

MOTHER: It's a lie, isn't it?

FATHER: You spend more than enough time with Jessica.

MOTHER: Well then why would she say it? I don't understand it.

FATHER: You want to know the reason? I can picture it exactly. She's in trouble at school. She's … I don't know, talked back, lied, done something. The teachers don't understand it. They take her aside. What a wonderful opportunity to put their amateur psychology to the test! They talk to her very seriously. "Jessica, what's wrong? Is everything alright at home?" And she sees – "aha! This is a way to get out of it."

MOTHER: Do you think so?

FATHER: Oh yes. They probably suggested it. "Do you spend enough time with your mother?" Wouldn't even consider asking about the father, the sexist pigs.

MOTHER: But what if it's not that?

FATHER: It is that. Don't you buy into this. You spend plenty of time with Jessica.

MOTHER: That's not what the school thinks.

FATHER: How the hell would they know?

MOTHER: Because they're with her all day!

FATHER: Everyone at that school is a total idiot.

MOTHER: Look, if Jessica really feels I neglect her then we've got a very big problem.

FATHER: Oh I don't believe this …

MOTHER: And I want to find out what it is without you standing there glaring at her the whole time.

Beat.

FATHER: Judy …

MOTHER: What?

FATHER: You have got to stop pandering to her.

MOTHER: What do you mean?

FATHER: You have got to stop pandering to her. I'm serious, Judy. That child will take and take and take until there's no more to give. And we have got to stop it. Now.

MOTHER: Well what am I supposed to do! Just let her hate me?

FATHER: She doesn't hate you.

MOTHER: Yes she does. Why else would she say it?

FATHER: Because she loves you. She wants you all the time. Remember when she was a baby? She'd cry every time you left the room for God's sake.

MOTHER: We don't know that's why she was crying.

FATHER: Oh please. It was obvious.

MOTHER: To you.

FATHER: This is the same thing. It's the same fucking thing all over again. She's not a baby anymore. She's a lot fucking smarter. This is just a tactic Judy. It's another tactic to get her own fucking way and I won't stand for it!

Pause.

MOTHER: But why is she like that? *(She is really asking.)* What have we done?

Beat.

FATHER: We haven't done anything.

MOTHER: Well obviously, Michael, we're doing something wrong because it is not normal for a ten-year-old child to go to her teachers and say she doesn't spend enough time with her mother! There's a problem!

FATHER: Yes, I think we do have a problem.

MOTHER: What is it?

FATHER: The problem is that our daughter is an attention-seeking little bitch!

MOTHER: Would you just keep your voice down?

FATHER: I don't give a shit if she hears me! I'm much more concerned about you.

Beat.

MOTHER: I try to be a good mother …

FATHER: You are a good mother.

MOTHER: Well apparently you're the only one who thinks so.

FATHER: Come on, Judy. You're wonderful with Jessica.

MOTHER: I do the best I can.

FATHER: Of course you do.

MOTHER: That's what I'll say. That I do the best I can. And it's not easy.

FATHER: I cannot believe they're sending over a social worker.

MOTHER: This is a nightmare.

FATHER: And you don't want me to shout at her. Unbelievable.

MOTHER: It won't help.

FATHER: Why the hell did you tell them it was alright to send this woman over? I thought it was just a suggestion.

MOTHER: What was I supposed to say? We're not going to look very good if we refuse to see her.

FATHER: Effectively, our daughter ... our daughter, has informed on us. And now they're sending the fucking authorities over. I mean this is fucking Kafka.

MOTHER: Then we'd better clean. Oh look! Some one's getting what they want.

FATHER: We're not cleaning.

MOTHER: I'll have to call the office first thing. I'm going to have to cancel a meeting. Two meetings. The timing couldn't actually be worse.

FATHER: I think we should call her up and tell her Monday isn't convenient.

MOTHER: No.

FATHER: Why?

MOTHER: Because it will look bad.

FATHER: Who gives a shit?

MOTHER: I do.

FATHER: Judy, listen to me. We haven't done anything wrong. We are under no obligation to impress this woman.

MOTHER: Yes we are. So do me a favour Michael and keep your temper when she comes over.

FATHER: Judy this is all a misunderstanding. It will be fine.

Beat.

Come on. You're just tired and you're upset.

MOTHER: Yes I am upset. I'm very upset.

FATHER: Me too.

MOTHER: I don't see why. You're not the one that's in trouble.

FATHER: Judy …

MOTHER: I mean how could this happen?

Beat.

I think she's angry I don't pick her up from school.

FATHER: You do pick her up. We pick her up all the time. Anyway it's only half an hour's walk with Anne-Marie for fuck's sake.

MOTHER: I spend all my time with her. I spend all the time I've got.

FATHER: I know.

MOTHER: I was in there tonight. I was in there for an hour. You got angry with me.

FATHER: I know.

MOTHER: I don't know what else to do. I play with her, I talk to her, I listen to her. I listen to her all the time.

FATHER: I know.

MOTHER: I just don't know what I've done wrong.

FATHER: You haven't done anything wrong.

MOTHER: My mother will be delighted.

FATHER: What's your mother got to do with anything?

MOTHER: It's what she always used to say to me. 'How will
you ever manage to bring up a child?' I'm not telling her.
I'm not fucking telling her.

FATHER: You're wonderful with Jessica.

MOTHER: You do not mention this to my parents.

FATHER: I won't.

MOTHER: Or anyone.

FATHER: I won't.

MOTHER: What if she says the same thing to this social
worker?

FATHER: You think she's going to do that? With us in the house?

MOTHER: I don't know if we can be there while they talk to her.

FATHER: Of course we're going to be there. I'm not leaving
my daughter alone with some woman we've never met
before who probably gets a bonus every time she sticks a
child in a home.

MOTHER: Well what if we have to?

FATHER: Then we should talk to Jessica before she sees her.

MOTHER: What should we say?

FATHER: We'll find out why she said what she said, tell her
as a result someone's coming over on Monday who wants
to put her in a home and explain that if she says it again
that's where she'll end up.

MOTHER: We can't say that.

FATHER: Why not? It's the truth.

MOTHER: Because we can't do that.

FATHER: She has to learn that what she says has consequences. That this isn't the fucking movies!

MOTHER: I have got to find out what's happening to her.

FATHER: Let's talk to her tonight.

MOTHER: I'm talking to her, by myself, tomorrow.

FATHER: She's my daughter too.

MOTHER: I don't care! I'm not going to be able to get anything out of her if you're there.

FATHER: Why the hell not?

MOTHER: Because she's scared of you.

FATHER: No she's not.

MOTHER: She is! She thinks you're going to spank her every five minutes!

FATHER: You're crazy ...

MOTHER: It's true.

FATHER: Bullshit. She just knows I don't let her get away with murder.

MOTHER: Well I'm sick of it.

FATHER: You're sick of it? Really?

Beat.

Well I won't stop her next time she bothers you when you're trying to work.

MOTHER: Fine.

FATHER: And you can make sure that she does her homework.

MOTHER: I do.

FATHER: Oh and she really listens to you. Do you know how many times a day I have to say 'listen to your mother'?

MOTHER: You just take over! You never give me a chance to discuss anything with her.

FATHER: It's not up for discussion. She has to do her homework.

MOTHER: You know, if you didn't scare her all the time it's quite possible that none of this would be happening.

FATHER: What?

MOTHER: What? You think this has nothing to do with you?

FATHER: Hey, the school is being ridiculous.

MOTHER: If she's unhappy at home it's not just because of me.

FATHER: She isn't unhappy at home but even if she was, I don't think it's very nice, Judy, to turn around and blame it all on me.

MOTHER: Well why should I be the one that takes all the blame!

FATHER: We haven't done anything. Neither of us have done anything.

MOTHER: Michael. It doesn't matter if we think we haven't done anything. What matters is that she feels she doesn't –

FATHER: She's ten years old.

MOTHER: So what?

FATHER: So what she feels is not an adult perspective.

MOTHER: Did you ever think that the reason that she said she doesn't spend enough time with me, is because she wants to get away from you?

Beat.

FATHER: Judy. That is really hurtful.

MOTHER: Well?

FATHER: No, I didn't think that at all.

MOTHER: Well I think it's perfectly possible.

FATHER: Why?

MOTHER: Because I know my daughter.

FATHER: Oh grow up! This is all just a competition. A competition about who can win.

MOTHER: Win what?

FATHER: Win whatever. What we eat for dinner, what we talk about while we're eating it, what we do when we've finished eating it. Win, win, win, that's all she wants. And you give into her every time.

MOTHER: What would you like me to do? Ignore her?

FATHER: It might be a start. Yes.

MOTHER: Then I'd have plenty of time for you.

FATHER: Oh I doubt the time you saved would go towards me. But I'm sure your clients would benefit hugely. You might make senior partner.

MOTHER: Well perhaps if I concentrated on work a little more, then you could concentrate on work a little more, instead of just sitting around the house criticizing everyone.

FATHER: Fuck you!

MOTHER: Michael!

FATHER: You have no idea how hard I'm working. I work my ass off in ways that you don't understand. That you don't begin to understand, that you don't try to understand.

MOTHER: Fine.

FATHER: I am working all the time, every day.

MOTHER: Then where's the book, Michael?

FATHER: Just because I don't write it down every second.

MOTHER: You don't write it down, no book.

FATHER: You want to do it? You want to write a novel? I'll do your job. I could have been a lawyer. And I'm sure that I, at least, would manage not to lose my files.

MOTHER: I don't want to write a novel, Michael. You do. Don't take it out on me just because you can't do it.

FATHER: I can do it.

MOTHER: Then where's the book?

FATHER: I'll write you a book.

MOTHER: Good. Get going.

FATHER: I'll write you a book and you won't like what's in it.

MOTHER: And I'll have you in court so fast it'll make your head spin, and believe me you'll be writing your next one living alone in some God- forsaken apartment you can barely afford unless you shut the fuck up!

A moment.

FATHER: I would love to see you manage without me. The dishwasher breaks, you call me in fucking tears.

Beat.

What the fuck was I supposed to do about it from New Orleans!

MOTHER: I have to get up early. I'm going to bed.

FATHER: Oh, yes, go to bed. Mustn't be late for the office.

MOTHER: Oh for God's sake, Michael. What do you want me to do? Stay home all day? Is that what you'd like?

A moment.

Is it? Is that what you and Jessica want?

FATHER: No.

MOTHER: Good! Because I won't do it!

FATHER: No one's saying don't work.

MOTHER: It's my job, Michael.

FATHER: You just want to make senior partner.

MOTHER: Of course I want to make senior partner. What's wrong with that? Wouldn't you? When you were writing your first book I hardly saw you.

FATHER: That was years ago.

MOTHER: And I hardly saw you. And I didn't mind.

FATHER: I bet you didn't.

MOTHER: I understood.

FATHER: I understand.

MOTHER: You just don't like it. When you were writing your
novel, properly writing it, I loved it. I loved supporting
you, and bringing you dinner at your desk, and I felt like
you were doing it for both of us.

FATHER: I was.

MOTHER: But you don't feel that way about me.

FATHER: You're not doing it for both of us.

MOTHER: Neither were you.

Beat.

FATHER: No one is more supportive of you that I am. I spend
hours helping you draft statements, don't I? And we talk
about your cases, and, my God, if it wasn't for me you
wouldn't have even applied for the job. It was me who
told you to go for the fucking thing.

MOTHER: Then why don't you let me do it?

FATHER: Because you disappear off into this little world that
I helped you build and then suddenly I'm not allowed in.
And I don't like it. I don't like feeling that there are parts
of the day that I am not allowed to make contact with you.

MOTHER: I'm working. It's normal to leave me alone. That
is how the rest of the world functions. Why, during every
step of the day, are you testing whether or not you are the
most important thing in my life?

FATHER: Because I need to know.

MOTHER: Well if you don't know by now … I mean it's
exhausting, Michael. It is absolutely exhausting. If you'd
just finish -

FATHER: Finish the book, finish the book. I can't! I can't get
Helena over to Portugal!

Beat.

MOTHER: Michael, you can.

Silence.

I'll talk to Jessica before I leave tomorrow morning. I'd be grateful if you didn't upset her about this before school.

FATHER: I love Jessica.

Beat.

I'll make it very clear to the social worker how much I love her. How's that?

MOTHER: Perfect.

FATHER: And we'll make sure the house is very clean, and we'll set you and Jessica in the kitchen by the stove, perhaps you could be braiding her hair, and I'll be very friendly, and you'll be charming, and we'll tell her how I read to Jessica and you sing to her, and Jessica can draw the woman some indecipherable pictures, and then off she'll go, never to be seen again. We'll pass with flying colors.

MOTHER: I don't think it will be quite that simple.

FATHER: Yes it will. If necessary I'll flirt. *(No reaction.)* Judy, it will be fine. Won't it? You know it will be fine.

MOTHER: I ought to tell them, Michael. About the hitting.

FATHER: Stop calling it that!

MOTHER: The spanking.

FATHER: Why?

MOTHER: Because it's relevant.

FATHER: To what?

44

MOTHER: To the situation.

FATHER: There's no situation. This is a mistake.

MOTHER: I think it's the right thing to do.

FATHER: How is it the right thing to do?

MOTHER: Well because you do hit her –

FATHER: I don't hit her, for Christ's sake -

MOTHER: And I think it affects Jessica's behavior.

FATHER: I'm sorry. I want to get this exactly straight. You're going to tell her, or wait and see if it comes up?

MOTHER: I imagine she'll ask.

FATHER: And what are you going to say?

MOTHER: Well nothing really. I'll just confirm that Jessica's not lying.

FATHER: But I don't think it's something you should bring up.

MOTHER: I think she should know.

FATHER: Why?

MOTHER: Because we all might benefit from talking some things through. This is an opportunity.

FATHER: To what?

MOTHER: To sort out our problems.

FATHER: What problems do we have? What problems did we have before tonight?

MOTHER: Look. Jessica's obviously not happy, I'm not happy.

FATHER: What do you mean you're not happy? You were happy before.

MOTHER: Let's just talk to this woman.

FATHER: I don't want to talk to this woman. I want to talk to you.

MOTHER: Michael, I've worked with social workers and they are usually very intelligent -

FATHER: Oh please.

MOTHER: Some are.

FATHER: I don't like people who's entire careers are built around where to allocate blame!

MOTHER: I'm going to tell her, Michael. I'm sorry.

Pause.

FATHER: On Monday morning, you're going to tell the social worker coming round to investigate our family, that I'm an unfit parent.

MOTHER: No I'm not.

FATHER: Oh yes you are. Because by telling her you're telling somebody who will immediately interpret it as that.

MOTHER: You haven't done anything you're ashamed of. Why are you so worried?

FATHER: Because if you bring it up then it will immediately have more significance than it actually has, won't it? And if Jessica's behavior is anything to go by, she will relish the opportunity to recount countless tales in which I lock her in the closet and beat her with an enormous stick.

MOTHER: I'll say she's lying.

FATHER: How do you know they'll believe you?

MOTHER: You really don't have any faith in the legal system, do you?

FATHER: Not enough to want to go on trial.

Beat.

MOTHER: Trials exist for a reason.

Beat.

FATHER: Hey guess what? I was going to back you up.

MOTHER: About what?

FATHER: They're coming here to talk about you, remember?

MOTHER: Well I'll tell them the truth.

FATHER: How about I tell them the truth?

MOTHER: You should tell them the truth.

FATHER: Alright. I'll tell them the reason Jessica is attention-seeking is that you have no attention to give to any of us.

MOTHER: Fine. You do that.

FATHER: That maybe Jessica feels like I do, every day. Second best.

MOTHER: You tell her, Michael.

FATHER: You're obsessed with your work!

MOTHER: Fine. Let it play itself out.

FATHER: And you spend no time with her at all!

MOTHER: If you do that I'll tell the social worker you beat the shit out of her.

Silence.

FATHER: I presume you want this to play itself out so that the two of us are still left with Jessica?

MOTHER: Yes.

FATHER: Right. Then why tell her anything at all? *(No response.)* You've never brought this up before. *(No response.)* I'll tell you what. I'll stop. She won't. You take over. What do you want to do with her the next time?

MOTHER: She'll have to go to her room.

FATHER: Great. You send her.

MOTHER: I will.

FATHER: And I'll sneak up in there with her and the two of us will have a secret little conference, like we're in a gang!

MOTHER: I can stop her allowance.

FATHER: I doubt she'd prefer that. More points for me.

MOTHER: It's not about what she'd prefer.

FATHER: Isn't it? I thought that's what all of this was about. What Jessica wants.

MOTHER: No. It's about what's best for her.

FATHER: And you think that's locking her up. Fine with me. We'll try it.

MOTHER: Look, I don't know! I don't know, Michael! How am I supposed to know? But someone's coming over and I think they might be of help. We sit down, we have a conversation and we sort it out.

FATHER: What makes you think they're on our side?

MOTHER: Well who's side do you think they're on?

FATHER: They're on the side of right. And if there's one thing we've learned about 'right,' it's that it isn't objective. In real life, right and wrong is not the preserve of one person or another. These people aren't interested in you, and they aren't interested in me, and they aren't interested in Jessica. They're interested in their own power, that they've built on their own fucking moral high-ground. And they are going to come in here and make pronouncements on a situation that they know next to nothing about –

MOTHER: But I want to know! I want to know, Michael!

Beat.

FATHER: You want to know what?

MOTHER: I want to know if I'm doing it right.

FATHER: How the hell are they going to know that?

MOTHER: They'll talk to Jessica. They'll talk to us. They're trained, Michael.

FATHER: What, in absolute truth?

MOTHER: They might not make pronouncements! It might just be suggestions.

FATHER: If there was a perfect way to bring up a child don't you think that someone might have published it in a little manual?

MOTHER: There's lots of different types of children.

FATHER: Oh I'm sure this woman has whittled it down to two categories: those who should be with their parents, and those who shouldn't.

MOTHER: It's not going to come down to that.

FATHER: How do you know? If you start this ball rolling who knows where it will end?

MOTHER: I know exactly where it will end. I'm white, I'm middle class and I earn in the upper tax bracket. Nobody's taking my daughter anywhere.

FATHER: Then why do this?

MOTHER: Because I need some support.

FATHER: Rallying the troops against me? Getting the army into position?

MOTHER: No Michael.

FATHER: I mean for God's sake, Judy! What do you want? Is this to punish me? To discipline me? Is that what you want? Little Michael to get the back of his legs slapped by a social worker? Is that what it will take for you to know that you're right?

MOTHER: Michael. Calm down.

FATHER: They won't stop with me. They'll move on to you. Are you ready for that?

MOTHER: They can't hurt us.

FATHER: Are you ready to listen to them tell you that perhaps you shouldn't have let me spank Jessica if you didn't like it?

MOTHER: I'm ready to listen.

FATHER: Listen to them tell you that Jessica would probably be happier if you were home all the time? Listen to them tell you that perhaps applying for senior partner at this evidently unsettling time for Jessica might not be the best thing for her psycho-social development?

MOTHER: If it's the right thing to do.

FATHER: And you'll do what they say?

MOTHER: That's not what I said. I said I would listen to what they had to say.

FATHER: Oh no. If we bring someone else in, there's no going back.

MOTHER: What's that supposed to mean?

FATHER: How seriously are you going to take them? What if they tell you I've been a bad father? What then? Will you divorce me? Or just throw it in my face every time we have a fight?

MOTHER: But you're not a bad father.

FATHER: They'll think you're just defending me, Judy.

MOTHER: Michael, they might tell us we're doing just fine. Imagine that. Can you imagine the relief?

Beat.

They're there anyway. They're watching anyway. The school is, now whoever they're sending. Let's just say what's been going on.

FATHER: How we bring up our child is about us. What matters is what you think. And what I think. Not what they think. This is a family. We're the authority. We make the rules.

MOTHER: Michael, I need something bigger than us! I just can't see through all of the discussion anymore.

FATHER: Then think harder.

MOTHER: I want to give them all the details.

Beat.

FATHER: Interesting, isn't it? Language. They. Them. Not us. They're not us.

MOTHER: No.

FATHER: Then I'm not enough for you.

MOTHER: Michael. Please. I'm too tired.

Silence. He looks at her.

FATHER: Would you die for me?

MOTHER: No, I wouldn't.

FATHER: Why?

MOTHER: Someone would have to be there for Jessica.

Beat.

FATHER: If you died for me, I'd be there for Jessica.

Pause.

I'd die for you. I would.

MOTHER: Alright. You look after Jessica, and I'll die for you. Happy?

FATHER: You haven't had to give up a single thing for this marriage, have you?

MOTHER: What?

FATHER: You haven't had to give anything up. And you wouldn't, would you? Not your files. Not your schedule. Not your life.

Pause.

MOTHER: Why should I? Why should either of us?

FATHER: No sense of loss.

MOTHER: We're not meant to lose anything. We're meant to gain. It's meant to be a gain. What do you feel like you've lost?

FATHER: Me. You.

MOTHER: Well we're here, aren't we?

FATHER: The door opens and other people come in to play with their rules and their games. I don't like their games. You do.

MOTHER: This isn't a game.

FATHER: I thought that the idea of marriage was that you built your own little world and it was over. That nobody bothered you anymore. That finally, you could just sit on the grass with your best friend and not be frightened that they were going to go away and make a new best friend, and not be frightened that you'd be left alone on the grass until they both came back again over to where you're sitting and kick your head in. I thought that you'd get to do everything together. That you'd get to enjoy everything together. And face everything together. Alone.

MOTHER: We do –

FATHER: It's funny. I've always known you didn't want that. I'd sense it every so often but I'd ignore it, push it away, or force you into it. I've seen myself, you know, make you give things up, bully you, beg you, beg you for attention. It's humiliating. And I spend nine minutes out of ten trying to force myself not to do it. But I usually lose the struggle. The way I love you I ... I look over at you making tea, or reading a book and I feel it charging through my body and I stand very still in case you see, and feel it as desperation. I honestly thought it would go away. After a couple of years. Settle down. But it hasn't. I don't think it ever will.

Beat.

MOTHER: I do love you too, you know?

FATHER: I think that you love me as much as anyone who isn't your flesh. I do. But they are two very different things. We love in two different ways. I can bear it. Most of the time. I can bear it. Most of the time. It's fine.

Silence. The MOTHER doesn't know what to say. The FATHER turns to leave.

I'm going downstairs.

MOTHER: Why?

FATHER: To work for a while.

MOTHER: Well that's good.

FATHER: Yes. Yes it is good, I suppose. I should cancel the painters. We won't want them here on Monday.

MOTHER: Thanks.

The FATHER turns to leave again.

I had an idea in the car. I thought we could ask my sister to give Jessica a few piano lessons before next semester. To see if she likes it.

FATHER: Oh let her play the trumpet if she wants to. Why not?

MOTHER: No, I agree. The piano's better.

FATHER: Sure. Fine.

The FATHER turns to leave again.

MOTHER: Good night.

He exits. The MOTHER sits there alone. She runs out of the room.

All's quiet.

Suddenly, the parents are back. Kissing. Pulling at each others clothes.
A desperate attempt to hang on to each other. They get to the bed.

End of play.

www.ingramcontent.com/pod-product-compliance
Ingram Content Group UK Ltd.
Pitfield, Milton Keynes, MK11 3LW, UK
UKHW020708280225
455688UK00012B/316